FREEDOM SUMMER 1964

TURNING POINT FOR VOTING RIGHTS

by Ngeri Nnachi

CAPSTONE PRESS
a capstone imprint

Spotlight is published by Capstone Press, an imprint of Capstone.
1710 Roe Crest Drive, North Mankato, Minnesota 56003
capstonepub.com

Library of Congress Cataloging-in-Publication Data is available on the Library of
Congress website.
ISBN: 9781669062097 (hardcover)
ISBN: 9781669062103 (paperback)
ISBN: 9781669062110 (ebook PDF)

Summary: Voting gives people a voice in their communities. In the past, racist laws and practices
kept Black American voices silent. No place was more affected by this racism than the state of
Mississippi. In 1964, organizers and volunteers brought change to Mississippi. This movement to
register Black voters became known as Freedom Summer, and it led to the passage of the Voting
Rights Act of 1965. Discover the people, events, and results of Freedom Summer, and learn why
voting rights remain an important issue today.

Editorial Credits
Editor: Erika L. Shores; Designer: Heidi Thompson; Media Researcher: Jo Miller;
Production Specialist: Tori Abraham

Image Credits
Alamy: Everett Collection Historical, 13; Associated Press, 10, BH, File, 23, Bill Hudson, 5, Jim
Bourdier, 16, Rogelio V. Solis, 19; Getty Images: Afro Newspaper/Gado, 24 (top), Ariel Skelley, 4
(top), Bettmann, 8, 20 (all), 25, Don Cravens, 11, Express, 12, Jackson State University, 7 (all), 14,
18 (all), Keystone, 24 (bottom), Michael Ochs Archives, 9, North Carolina Central University, 21,
PhotoQuest, 15, Robert Elfstrom/Villon Films, 17; Shutterstock: Andrey_Popov, 4 (middle), ang
intaravichian, background (throughout), Jorge Salcedo, 4 (bottom), Trevor Bexon, 27, Veja, Cover,
design element (throughout); Wikimedia/Yoichi Okamoto, 26

TABLE OF CONTENTS

GIVING EVERYONE A VOICE

Your vote is your voice. What does that mean? It means voting in elections gives people a say in what happens in their communities. One goal of the U.S. government system is that everyone has a voice. But that hasn't always happened. In this country, some voices have not been heard.

In the 1960s, Black Americans had a legal right to vote. But white people in many states worked hard to make sure Black people did not vote. They made Black people pass difficult tests to prevent them from voting. They also scared Black people who tried to vote. Sometimes police arrested them. Other times bosses fired Black people from their jobs.

By 1964, a Mississippi activist named Robert Moses believed if white people from other parts of the country spoke up, others would pay attention. So he launched a plan.

Civil rights activists protested for voting rights outside the courthouse in Greenwood, Mississippi, in March 1964.

Hundreds of volunteers would spend the summer in Mississippi. They would set up Black schools. They would register Black people to vote.

Many local white people didn't like the plan. They said terrible things to the volunteers. They started fires at the Black schools. They chased volunteers with their cars and sometimes beat them up. Local white people even killed some of the volunteers. But the volunteers' work did make voting easier and safer for African Americans. This season of activism became known as Freedom Summer.

THINK MORE ABOUT IT!

Imagine your school is buying new outdoor equipment. The principal says students can vote to decide between a climbing wall or a basketball court. The principal made a rule, though. Only students who can pass a difficult math test are allowed to vote. Is this rule fair? Why or why not?

Coordinator for the Freedom Schools, Liz Fusco (far left), helped organize volunteers and taught Black Mississippians about their voting rights.

FACT

People in the United States choose their leaders. Someone who wants to be president or mayor can run for office. During an election, people vote. In most states, people must register before they are allowed to vote.

CHAPTER 1

UNFAIRNESS IN THE SOUTH

The United States has a long history of not letting everyone vote for their leaders. When the country formed, only white men who owned land could vote. After the Civil War (1861–1865), an amendment to the Constitution gave Black men the right to vote. But in many states, especially in the South, white people made rules to stop Black people from voting. These white people believed Black people should not have the same rights. They believed Black people should not have a say in what happened in their communities.

Segregation kept Black people and white people apart on buses.

FACT

Before the Civil War, most Black people in the South were enslaved. White people treated enslaved Black people as their property. They forced enslaved people to do hard work for no pay.

In the 1950s and 1960s, local rules stopped African Americans from voting in Mississippi. One rule was that a person had to pay money, called a poll tax, to vote. Most Black people in Mississippi couldn't afford a tax.

Discrimination against Black people happened every day across the South. Jim Crow laws said Black people and white people couldn't share public services. Black people had to sit at the back of buses, while white people sat in front. A Black person had to stand if a white person wanted their seat. Black children and white children went to different schools. The schools for white children were usually nicer, with better books and buildings.

MEDGAR EVERS

In Mississippi, Medgar Evers grew up seeing cruelty against Black people. Soon after his World War II (1939–1945) army service, he registered to vote in his home state. But when he and other former soldiers tried to vote in a 1946 election, white people stopped them.

Evers joined the National Association for the Advancement of Colored People (NAACP), a group that works to stop racial discrimination. And as a traveling insurance agent, Evers started local chapters of the NAACP in Mississippi. He organized protests and voter registration drives, as well as fighting against Jim Crow laws. Evers was shot to death outside his home in 1963, the year before Freedom Summer.

Racism and discrimination created violence as well. Some white people were known to destroy Black people's property and fire Black people from jobs. Racist white police officers felt free to beat Black people and put them in jail. This was especially true if those Black people were doing something white people disagreed with, such as trying to vote. Black people fought back against this treatment. But no one would stop or punish a white person who beat or shot a Black person. And because white people made the laws, it was hard for Black people to change them.

Rosa Parks arrives at the courthouse on February 24, 1956. She had been arrested and fined for not giving up her seat on a segregated bus.

In 1956, civil rights leader Dr. Martin Luther King Jr. was arrested for his involvement in the Montgomery Bus Boycott.

By the 1950s, Black people were working together to push back. One day in 1955, in Montgomery, Alabama, a Black woman named Rosa Parks took a bus home from work. When the bus driver told her to give up her seat, she said, "No." Police arrested Parks, kicking off a huge protest. For more than a year, Black people in Montgomery stopped riding buses. Eventually, the Supreme Court ruled having separate bus sections was illegal. This was just one small part of the Civil Rights Movement growing across the South.

CHAPTER 2

BRINGING CHANGE TO MISSISSIPPI

Fannie Lou Hamer grew up in Mississippi. Her family lived and worked on a plantation, a big farm owned by white people. Her family picked cotton as payment for living there. They never earned much money. Hamer went to school a little bit, but she did not learn about politics or voting. Black farm workers didn't usually have radios or newspapers. They didn't know about voting rights. In 1962, when she was 44 years old, Hamer learned she had a right to vote.

A volunteer for the Student Nonviolent Coordinating Committee stands outside the group's headquarters in Atlanta.

FACT

Literacy tests were made to be nearly impossible to pass for Black people who were trying to register to vote.

A group called the Student Nonviolent Coordinating Committee (SNCC) was working hard to register Black people to vote. It wasn't easy. Hamer and 17 others traveled to their county office to try to register. Officials allowed only Hamer and one other traveler to take the required literacy test. Both failed. They were not allowed to register.

A group waiting to register to vote at a Mississippi courthouse

When Hamer got home, the plantation owner fired her for trying to register. He also took her family's car and other belongings. That may seem hard to believe. At the time, most local police and officials didn't think Black people should vote. They took the plantation owner's side. They didn't think Black people should have the same rights as white people. Few who had power to punish a white person wanted to help a Black person. Hamer knew the unfairness needed to change. She started working for SNCC, helping people register to vote.

Members of SNCC went to people's homes to talk to them about registering to vote.

The bus boycott in Montgomery wasn't the only civil rights protest. In Greensboro, North Carolina, Black people protested by sitting in whites-only lunch cafes. Another group protested by riding buses that crossed state lines. This group was known as the Freedom Riders. Federal law said Black and white people could sit together on buses. It said Black people had the right to use bus stations as well. But when Freedom Riders did these things, white people attacked them. Protests brought attention to segregation along with court cases that ruled against the unfair practices.

FANNIE LOU HAMER

In 1962, Fannie Lou Hamer happened to attend a meeting at her church. Hearing the speakers talk about voting would change her life. She decided this was a cause she wanted to work toward. So she registered voters and educated her neighbors. Hamer led her county's SNCC chapter and helped Robert Moses plan Freedom Summer. She became known for singing spirituals and her powerful way of speaking. Hamer stayed an activist for the rest of her life.

In Mississippi, activists focused on voting. They believed if Black people could help choose their leaders, white people would have to treat them better. In 1964, Mississippi had more than 450,000 African Americans of voting age, but only 16,000 of them were registered to vote.

Reverend Donald Tucker (left) leading a group of Black voters to register at the courthouse in Greenwood, Mississippi.

Robert Moses had been leading the SNCC's voter registration in Mississippi for several years. He thought it would help if people outside the state understood what was happening there. He knew if Northerners found out how Southern white people treated Black people, they would be angry. He also believed if Northern white people spoke up, the media and government would pay attention. White volunteers from wealthy families and universities would make national news.

ROBERT MOSES

Robert Parris Moses grew up in Harlem, New York, and became a math teacher. As an activist, he helped SNCC and the Southern Christian Leadership Conference (SCLC). Moses also led the Council of Federated Organizations (COFO), a group of activist organizations working together, and was the main coordinator of Freedom Summer.

Moses was a quiet organizer, not known for big speeches. One of his strengths was teaching new civil rights leaders, including Fannie Lou Hamer. Most historians agree Freedom Summer would not have happened without him.

CHAPTER 3

SUMMER OF VIOLENCE AND FEAR

Volunteers from the North met Moses, Hamer, and other Black activists in Ohio for training in June. Most of the volunteers were white college students, both male and female. Moses and others believed white people and Black people had to work together to make things better in Mississippi.

The volunteers learned how to register voters, build schools, and teach young Black students. Those were the main goals of the Freedom Summer project.

FLONZIE BROWN WRIGHT

Wright in 2016

Flonzie Brown Wright grew up in Canton, Mississippi. When she was 12 years old, white men killed two of her teenage cousins. After Medgar Evers was killed, she began working with the NAACP, and she helped thousands of Black people register to vote.

During Freedom Summer, six volunteers stayed with Wright and her young children. In the evenings, she played guitar and they all sang together, building strength and courage for the next day of hard work. In 1968, she became the first African American woman elected to public office in Mississippi, joining the board of election commissioners.

The training was also about safety in Mississippi. White people in Mississippi didn't want Northerners around. They didn't want Black people to vote. They were against Freedom Summer. Locals might point guns at Black people or at white people who were friendly with them. Locals were likely to chase and attack out-of-towners. One rule for volunteers was to never go anywhere alone. Going out at night was not allowed at all. The activists worked hard to explain how dangerous it could be to help Black people in Mississippi.

The volunteers stayed in the homes of Black residents. They slept on floors of tiny shacks. They shared meals, music, and conversation with their hosts.

Local white people were angry about the volunteers. They set fire to churches and other buildings planned as Freedom Schools. Groups of white men in pickup trucks chased Black people and any white people who helped them, sometimes beating or even shooting them.

Three activists left the Ohio training early. James Chaney, Andrew Goodman, and Michael Schwerner traveled to Longdale, Mississippi, to investigate a church burning. Following the COFO safety rules, the activists promised to be back by 4:00 in the afternoon on June 21. The men did not return, and COFO members began to look for them.

Andrew Goodman

James Chaney

Michael Schwerner

TAKE ACTION!

Ask your family if you can attend or listen to a meeting of your school board, parks board, or city council. Think about how the discussion affects your school, park, or city. Being informed will help you when you're old enough to vote.

The search would last for 44 days. The FBI finally found the men's beaten bodies buried under an earthen dam. The murders of the three activists brought national attention to Mississippi. People around the country were shocked at the violence against Black people and civil rights activists in Mississippi.

DICK GREGORY

Dick Gregory was a popular comedian and a civil rights activist in the 1960s. In 1962, Medgar Evers asked Gregory to come to an NAACP voter registration drive. Evers hoped such a big name would spark interest.

In June 1964, when Goodman, Chaney, and Schwerner disappeared, Gregory went to Mississippi right away. He traveled with other civil rights activists to look for the missing men. He also raised money to offer a reward for useful information. Many activists give Gregory credit for keeping media attention on the case until it was solved.

Ten years before Freedom Summer, the Supreme Court had ruled on *Brown v. Board of Education*. The court said it was illegal to have separate Black and white schools.

In Mississippi, this court case had mostly been ignored. Public schools there still did not serve white and Black students equally. Black students went to schools with few resources.

Freedom Summer volunteers helped set up 41 schools in churches, yards, and even old outhouses. Then the volunteers taught reading, writing, and math. They also taught about Black history, the civil rights movement, and voting. Students included young children, teenagers, and adults of all ages.

THINK MORE ABOUT IT!

Think about the supplies and resources at your school. If you were going to help at a school that had fewer resources, what do you think would be useful? What subjects would you focus on? Why?

A Freedom Summer volunteer teaches students at a Freedom School in Jackson, Mississippi.

CHAPTER 4

VOTING RIGHTS THEN AND NOW

The 1964 Democratic National Convention would choose candidates to run in the upcoming election. Mississippi activists knew those people would be white. Freedom Summer activists found their own candidates who would care about Mississippi's poor Black people. They formed the Mississippi Freedom Democratic Party (MFDP).

The MFDP chose 68 people to stand for Mississippi, including Fannie Lou Hamer. The convention leaders didn't accept any of them. But the MFDP's efforts inspired other African Americans to register to vote.

Fannie Lou Hamer speaking to a reporter in 1964

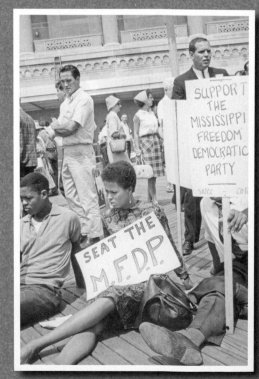

Protesters at the 1964 Democratic National Convention

Protesters at the 1964 Democratic National Convention demanded that members of the Mississippi Freedom Democratic Party represent the state.

Freedom Summer brought attention to Mississippi. Journalists wrote stories for national newspapers. TV news shared the story of the three missing activists. Readers and viewers didn't like what they saw. They asked elected officials to stop the violence.

Volunteers wrote letters home to their families. Their worried parents contacted their local governments and the president, asking them for help.

Finally, on August 6, 1965, President Lyndon Johnson signed the Voting Rights Act. Most historians agree Freedom Summer and other civil rights activism helped make this law happen. The law made literacy tests illegal and said federal officials could look into poll taxes in local elections. It also said federal groups could watch local elections, to make sure people could vote safely and fairly.

The Voting Rights Act made a difference. By 1969, 59 percent of African Americans voted in Mississippi. It was a huge increase from the 6 percent who voted in 1964.

Dr. Martin Luther King Jr. (right, center) and other civil rights leaders look on as President Lyndon Johnson (left) signs the Voting Rights Act.

TAKE ACTION!

Think about a cause that's important to you. Do you care about homeless animals? Or maybe you feel strongly about climate change. Find ways to get involved! Are there groups in your community already working for change? Attend a meeting. Talk to classmates. You could start your own group.

The United States still has rules about who can vote. A person must be a U.S. citizen and at least 18 years old. In many places, people must be registered by a state deadline. In most states, someone who has been found guilty of certain crimes cannot vote.

Still today, some states are passing laws that make it hard for everyone to vote. In some places, every voter must show their identification (ID) at their polling place. But if the name or address on someone's ID doesn't match their registration, they may not be allowed to vote. That could affect someone who recently moved or someone without a permanent home. Some people have a difficult time even getting to the places that issue IDs.

Some people still don't want certain people to vote, especially if they want different officials to be elected. They try to trick or scare someone who might vote differently. It's not legal, but it happens. And sometimes there aren't enough polling places in an area for everyone to vote easily. Voters may have to wait in long lines for their turn. If voting is too hard, some people won't do it.

Freedom Summer was a turning point for society. Volunteers of different ages, races, and backgrounds were united in their cause for change. Many who traveled to Mississippi left the world better than they found it. Some gave up their lives to fight for the basic rights of African Americans. Freedom Summer brought people together for a common good: the right to vote freely in one's own community. While this movement made progress, the fight for voting rights and equality continues today.

TIMELINE OF VOTING RIGHTS

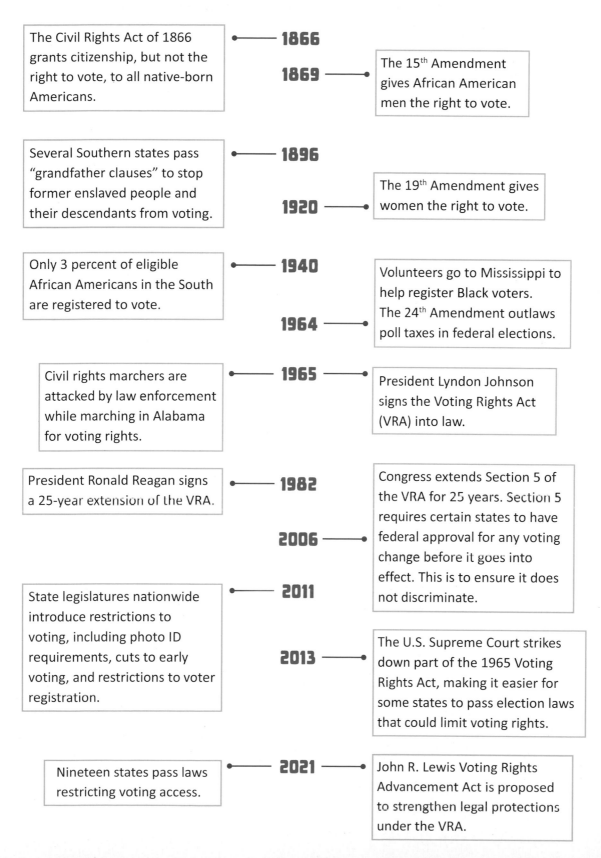

1866
The Civil Rights Act of 1866 grants citizenship, but not the right to vote, to all native-born Americans.

1869
The 15th Amendment gives African American men the right to vote.

1896
Several Southern states pass "grandfather clauses" to stop former enslaved people and their descendants from voting.

1920
The 19th Amendment gives women the right to vote.

1940
Only 3 percent of eligible African Americans in the South are registered to vote.

1964
Volunteers go to Mississippi to help register Black voters. The 24th Amendment outlaws poll taxes in federal elections.

1965
Civil rights marchers are attacked by law enforcement while marching in Alabama for voting rights.

President Lyndon Johnson signs the Voting Rights Act (VRA) into law.

1982
President Ronald Reagan signs a 25-year extension of the VRA.

2006
Congress extends Section 5 of the VRA for 25 years. Section 5 requires certain states to have federal approval for any voting change before it goes into effect. This is to ensure it does not discriminate.

2011
State legislatures nationwide introduce restrictions to voting, including photo ID requirements, cuts to early voting, and restrictions to voter registration.

2013
The U.S. Supreme Court strikes down part of the 1965 Voting Rights Act, making it easier for some states to pass election laws that could limit voting rights.

2021
Nineteen states pass laws restricting voting access.

John R. Lewis Voting Rights Advancement Act is proposed to strengthen legal protections under the VRA.

GLOSSARY

activist (AK-tuh-vist)—a person who works to make changes in the world, often by speaking out or protesting

candidate (KAN-duh-dayt)—a person running for office in an election

discrimination (dis-kri-muh-NAY-shuhn)—unfair treatment toward a person or group, especially based on race, ethnicity, age, gender, or ability

Jim Crow laws (JIM KROH LAWZ)—state and local laws that kept Black people separate from white people and took rights away from African Americans

literacy test (LIT-uh-ruh-cee TEST)—a written exam that checked whether a person could read and write, but was designed to be nearly impossible to pass; historically used to stop African Americans from becoming registered voters

spiritual (SPIHR-uh-choo-uhl)—a religious folk song started by African Americans in the South

READ MORE

Armand, Glenda. *Black Leaders in the Civil Rights Movement*. Emeryville, CA: Rockridge Press, 2021.

Lewis, Cicely. *Focus on Civil Rights Sit-Ins.* Minneapolis: Lerner Publications, 2023.

Tyner, Artika R. *The Untold Story of Sarah Keys Evans: Civil Rights Soldier*. North Mankato, MN: Capstone Press, 2023.

INTERNET SITES

Atlanta History Center: Civil Rights Toolkit
atlantahistorycenter.com/learning-research/learning-lab/civil-rights-toolkit/

Ben's Guide to the U.S. Government
bensguide.gpo.gov/learning-adventures-14more?id=36&age=ben4_8

History for Kids: Civil Rights Movements
historyforkids.net/civil-rights.html

INDEX

ABOUT THE AUTHOR

Ngeri Nnachi is an activist, educator, and scholar with a focus on social justice and equity. She loves working with children in building their literacy and leadership skills. In her spare time, she can be found visiting critical civil rights spaces and sewing bright, vibrant fabrics into fun items.